The Beautiful Garden of Eden

written by Gary Bower | illustrated by Barbara Chotiner

TYNDALE
KIDS

Tyndale House Publishers, Inc.
Carol Stream, IL

To Maylin Jo

Visit Tyndale's website for kids at www.tyndale.com/kids.

Visit Gary Bower online at www.bowerarts.com.

TYNDALE is a registered trademark of Tyndale House Publishers, Inc. The Tyndale Kids logo is a trademark of Tyndale House Publishers, Inc.

The Beautiful Garden of Eden

Designed by Jacqueline L. Nuñez

Edited by Sarah Rubio

Scripture quotations are taken from the *Holy Bible*, New Living Translation, copyright © 1996, 2004, 2015 by Tyndale House Foundation. Used by permission of Tyndale House Publishers, Inc., Carol Stream, Illinois 60188. All rights reserved.

For manufacturing information regarding this product, please call 1-800-323-9400.

Library of Congress Cataloging-in-Publication Data

Names: Bower, Gary, date, author.
Title: The beautiful garden of Eden / Gary Bower.
Description: Carol Stream, Illinois : Tyndale House Publishers, Inc., [2017]
  | Series: Faith that God built | Audience: Age 4-7. | Audience: Grade K to
  Grade 3.
Identifiers: LCCN 2016010621 | ISBN 9781496417435 (hc)
Subjects: LCSH: Eden--Juvenile literature.
Classification: LCC BS1237 .B69 2017 | DDC 222/.1109505--dc23 LC record available at https://lccn.loc.gov/2016010621

Printed in China

23	22	21	20	19	18	17
7	6	5	4	3	2	1

This is the **Garden of Eden.**

1

These are **the trees that swayed in the breeze** in the beautiful **Garden of Eden.**

This is **the tree that caused the upheaval,**

the tree of the knowledge of good and of evil,

That grew with **the trees that swayed in the breeze**
in the beautiful **Garden of Eden.**

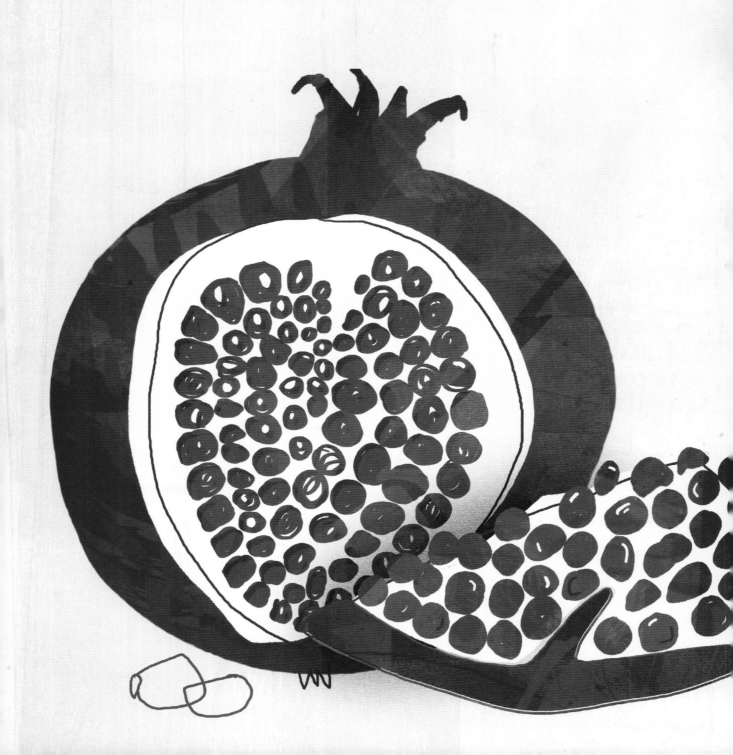

This is **the fruit, so slurpy and sweet,**

that God warned His gardeners never to eat,

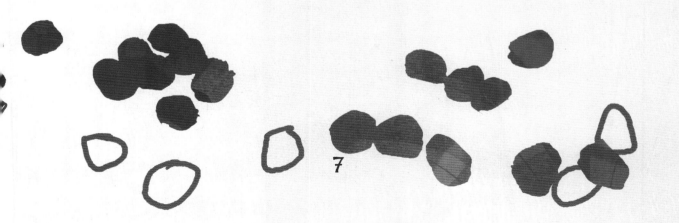

7

8

Plucked from **the tree that caused the upheaval,** the tree of the knowledge of good and of evil,

That grew with **the trees that swayed in the breeze** in the beautiful **Garden of Eden.**

This guy is **Adam, the very first man,**

  molded from mud when Creation began,

Who ate of **the fruit, so slurpy and sweet,**

  that God warned His gardeners never to eat,

Plucked from **the tree that caused the upheaval,** the tree of the knowledge of good and of evil,

That grew with **the trees that swayed in the breeze** in the beautiful **Garden of Eden.**

This woman is **Eve, so comely and cute,** who
    bit it the minute she handled the fruit,
Then gave it to **Adam, the very first man,**
    molded from mud when Creation began,

15

Who ate of **the fruit, so slurpy and sweet,** that God
warned His gardeners never to eat,
Plucked from **the tree that caused the upheaval,**

the tree of the knowledge of good and of evil,
That grew with **the trees that swayed in
the breeze** in the beautiful **Garden of Eden.**

This is **the serpent** who stooped to deceive, and damage the Garden by lying to Eve—

18

Gullible Eve, so comely and cute,

who bit it the minute she handled the fruit,

Then gave it to **Adam, the very first man,** molded
from mud when Creation began,
Who ate of **the fruit, so slurpy and sweet,**
that God warned His gardeners never to eat,

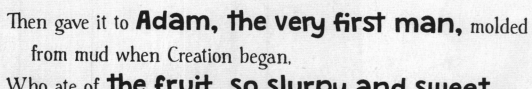

20

Plucked from **the tree that caused the upheaval,** the tree of the knowledge of good and of evil, That grew with **the trees that swayed in the breeze** in the beautiful **Garden of Eden.**

This is **the crushing, calamitous curse** that made
the world wayward and woefully worse,
Because of **the serpent** who stooped to deceive, and damage
the Garden by lying to Eve—

Gullible Eve, so comely and cute, who bit it the minute she handled the fruit,
Then gave it to **Adam, the very first man,** molded from mud when Creation began,
Who ate of **the fruit, so slurpy and sweet,** that God warned His gardeners never to eat,

Plucked from **the tree that caused the upheaval,**
the tree of the knowledge of good and of evil,
That grew with **the trees that swayed in the breeze** in the beautiful **Garden of Eden.**

25

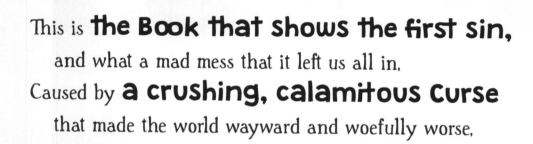

This is **the Book that shows the first sin,**
and what a mad mess that it left us all in,
Caused by **a crushing, calamitous Curse**
that made the world wayward and woefully worse,

26

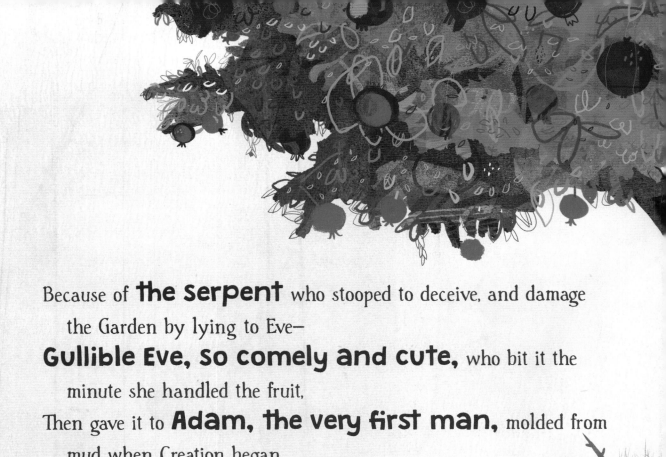

Because of **the serpent** who stooped to deceive, and damage
the Garden by lying to Eve—

Gullible Eve, so comely and cute, who bit it the
minute she handled the fruit,

Then gave it to **Adam, the very first man,** molded from
mud when Creation began,

Who ate of **the fruit, so slurpy and sweet,**
that God warned His gardeners never to eat,

Plucked from **the tree that caused the upheaval,** the tree of the knowledge of good and of evil, That grew with **the trees that swayed in the breeze** in the beautiful **Garden of Eden.**

For the whole story,
see Genesis 1–3.

Christ has rescued
us from the curse.

GALATIANS 3:13